DAM RATS
Smears and Virtue Signaling

by Karen Kellock Ph.D.

Manual for Superior Men

A complete theory based on Einstein physics,
Political Psychology, Systems Theory
and Archetypal Psychiatry.

FORMULA

All success attraction
All disease obstruction
All recovery elimination

You must fast on all three

OBSTRUCTIONS:

People
Habit
Food

DAM RATS

Smears and Virtue Signaling

Systems Theory: how the system creates/maintains pathology in the one: the identified patient seen as scum. There's always an altercation right before becoming famous and rich. It's like the test, rejecting the witch. To see behind the mask is an incredibly beneficial task. To get to success divide from old systems keeping you down. If you fit you're illegit. If you don't it may mean you're God's kid. It's New Age to be positive: thinking everything's ok when it isn't. The past holds us down: let it go, it was just a scaffold while growing a crown. Never throw your pearls before swine or be trampled by em. They don't just snub, they ruin.

RATS, VENOM & BEGGIN'

FACE THE PIT TO GET OVER IT
HE ROBBED YOUR IDENTITY
THE FALSE CHURCH
PLAYING CHURCH
GOD VS. TRADITIONS OF MEN

RATS, VENOM & BEGGIN'

FACE THE PIT TO GET OVER IT

It'll be horrible to face that--your dire period of enslavement--but you must for freedom.

Divine fun: You may roll the boulder up a hill 90% then God takes over and suddenly you're done.

You're a genius, so now BE your genius and get offa this thing about shame inherited but erased see.

If I fire someone and don't know why, I don't have to know why. Trust all instincts if sober, aye.

The original shamers are gone, the others passed it down for fun and it all landed on you, the chump.

When you finally get to success you're too old for their attention anyway but it got you there ok.

Ask yourself: WHY is he circling back? It's about availability, making sure of it as a fact.

Accept present emptiness as a sign of complete happiness after the transition to bliss.

HE ROBBED YOUR IDENTITY

You're already in the cage, it's no fun "getting" you. It's all in the chase with a fickle narcissist Sue.

A narcissist takes who you are: your identity, dreams and goals afar. Get you back by leaving the narc.

Hypersensitivity to sounds after bad relationship is the body's adaptation to acquire survival tips.

RATS, VENOM & BEGGIN'

If you both need help he will help the stranger first. The reason is a source of new supply of course.

Their altruism is for the intention of fooling others not to uplift em, remember that always friend.

A narcissist is into the chase: getting them, influencing them and deluding them for admiration.

Dog parks are INSANE. At least one dog is killed every day as ferocious fights are inevitable ok.

THE FALSE CHURCH

The false church is all about tolerance, acceptance and keeping the peace. That's not Christian see.

As soon as the "Christian band" becomes popular and rich they lose their standards inch by inch.

"Continue to find peace and YOUR truth" is the welcome mat to demonic heresies too.

A jumble of words with zero truth, zero God's message and nothing but a social massage: the FALSE.

These are "cum bay-yah" churches. They replace the old hymns with new ones on social graces.

The minute I walked through that church door I hated it but you didn't, you loved it didn't you dear.

PLAYING CHURCH

These people are PLAYING church. Just like they play at everything, from God's word divorced.

They insist you go to their pot lucks as if its God. If you're not social you are godless and odd.

RATS, VENOM & BEGGIN'

To have a spiritual revelation and then to be cut down by going to a church is sad and confusion.

Church wasn't a lamp to guide but a brick to carry. Made-up requirements of humans, heresies.

God is loving and comforting to me but in the false church I felt I was in [social] alien territory.

If you wouldn't hang out with them you didn't love God. That's the line of bull I saw through right off.

GOD VS. THE TRADITIONS OF MEN

Whenever you see "social justice" in the church, escape that pit--the devil has taken over the script.

That's false religion: man's traditions. It is the traditions of men obstructing the true God.

It is the traditions of men that obstruct scientific revelation also. It's always a blinder ya know.

Scientific discoverers defy tradition also. They were usually Christian, a fact few discuss or know.

Christianity comes from God--the Word--not the traditions of men but that's how it is friend.

They're always trying to merge tradition with modern for maximum approval and that's the devil.

As soon as they make money or attract fans they lean into collective beliefs and not God's plan.

"He wasn't compromising, he was just saying what Jesus woulda said". Now it's worldly instead.

When you dare to escape you're met with shock and rage. Fence up for they'll take revenge ok.

DAM RATS
ADAPTING TO A NARCISSIST

DAM RATS
ADAPTING TO A NARCISSIST

The first strategy dealing with narcissists is to know thyself so when discard comes you stay well.

The second strategy is know your own emotions: don't accept what he projects or drown in them.

Don't expect reciprocity when dealing with a narcissist. They have no empathy, they're not sensitive.

He tends to be envious, so limit you accomplishments and talents in front of the narcissist.

Let go of all prideful fantasy about changing the narcissist or getting even/it's not happening.

DON'T EVOKE HIS RAGE

Don't evoke his jealousy and thus narcissistic rage. Keep your cards close to your chest ok.

He's so invested in keeping the grandiose, entitled, arrogant boat afloat don't try getting back.

Everyday life tends to ground us and make us more mature: the narcissist lacks this for sure.

The trick is to walk away gently with a poker face and get loving help right away: good luck, KK.

Don't waste time getting even. Just harden your boundaries and self-awareness, moving on.

Don't focus energy since it becomes obsessive, your whole world focused on his petty business.

ADAPTING TO A NARCISSIST RAT

He's so unpredictable any focus will take up all your time and utterly destroy your tired mind.

Don't let him know you're obsessed because that feeds his supply: he'd love to know about it, aye.

Cognitive architecture, core beliefs and self image of narcissists: we now further investigate this.

Spill your mind to husband, boyfriend or a man who's committed to you not a narcissist in lieu.

NARCISSISTS ARE PURE TROUBLE

We learn this to understand the strife--pure havoc--the narcissist creates in other people's lives.

The core passion that drives narcissism is ENVY, a primitive emotion and form of hatred see.

Envy for him is an excruciating feeling of inner lack. He wants to take from other/destroy him in fact.

An internal sense of lack making him want to destroy what other's have: talents, things, suave.

And to think you had a soul tie with this person! What a vacillating universe you've been living in.

Aspire to the level of Trump and all these other troublemakers, dump: transcend this crud.

He asks favors he has no right asking, you always feel in a bind or a sense of hurt confusion's lurking.

Others have something perceived as good and worthy, so he seeks to destroy it: get that honey.

He's vindictive: withdraw before he triggers jealousy as he surely will because you're intelligent.

ADAPTING TO A NARCISSIST RAT

He's vindictive: because you're better, walk away gently before he targets you with his rage sister.

You're not dealing with appreciator but a mimicker and supply getter followed by discarder.

NARCISSISTIC [PATHOLOGICAL] ENVY

Don't respond if he hoovers back or you'll relapse by losing yourself and all happiness in fact.

Men are envious of rich and famous women but add narcissistic envy = she needs protection.

This envy is tantamount to a firstborn's rage at the new baby: tantrums, acting out or bedwetting.

A painful inner sense that I have been dethroned, shown to be inferior, a has-been or whatever.

Since inherited shame fell on you it's all you think about: what a terrible person you are/a nut.

You see all in a negative light about yourself back then, when that's how shame forms perception.

The infant panics the exact same way: I can't get my parents love in the same way anymore ok.

NOT TO GET EVEN BUT DESTROY

Envy for him becomes a compulsive need to destroy all that which is good, beautiful or superior.

His experience of envy is largely unconscious and comes out as contempt for worthless trash.

Thru disdain the narc neutralizes his feelings of envy, by treating the envied target with contempt.

ADAPTING TO A NARCISSIST RAT

He can become incredibly regressed and unhinged, a dangerous person when fully engaged.

Modern western culture is more individualistic than ever in power choice and agency: not groupies.

Positive masculine and feminine energy acts as a magnet: a polarity of magnetism/chemistry.

There's an emergence of masculine energy in women across all domains of life: they're prickly.

DOMINANCE IN FEMALES

Dominance, strength, toughness, determination: these are the attributes now shoved on women.

Striving for complete self-sufficiency works against the emergence of receptive feminine energy.

The need to be tough all the time is exhausting to feminine energy and ruins relationships see.

The sexual marketplace hinges on the polarity between feminine and masculine so she loses by this.

With women going masculine there is no more magnetism in this polarity, a real shame honey.

Exploitative, tyrannical and self-serving is the corrupted, shadow form of masculinity.

The dark triad is Machiavellianism and psychopathy with narcissism: it's the new social trend.

Women give sexual preference to dark triad traits while having no magnetism with a nice guy ok.

POOR HEALTH INCREASES DEVALUATION

ADAPTING TO A NARCISSIST RAT

Put chronic inflammation with slowed metabolism and you get spellbound: trapped/cause unknown.

Weight gain, diabetes and high blood pressure are all common being locked into a narc for years.

Deteriorating health of the empath is used as an excuse to devaluate them further, of course.

People know what they did the minute they did it but it's too late by then, the alert exactly read em.

Goal: improve physical health, break free of spellbinding effect, focus on body not others.

He is self-insulated/very resistant to feedback from the environment: for this reason he can't evolve.

END OF FREEDOM OR BEGIN AGAIN

Americana: A system so good everyone adopted it willingly. Protestors are bought/divorced from reality.

Now we've won, our real work starts: Re-educate dumbed public, teach kids Civics and warm stony hearts.

Hollywood has lost all class. It's now a promoter of globalism and taking our guns but not theirs: the brass.

The Biden years are terrible: Waking up every morning with dread, fearing we'd end in a camp or dead.

Renaissance is about flowering of the free human will. It built America but liberals want to kill it still?

Under Trump more than half didn't pay taxes. Such a bad man, isn't he? The anti-Trumpists, asses.

HOLLYWOOD SCUM DIVIDE THE COUNTRY

ADAPTING TO A NARCISSIST RAT

Hollywood scum trying to divide this country say "whites are inherently bad/racist": This is the bigotry.

It's not just about Trump but the last 40 years of being on the begging end with liberal arrogance/intransigence.

Politics has split families for 40 years--conservatives became the black sheep: alone, bewildered and in tears.

Revive the incredible American dynamo: No taxes for working people, not letting globalists sell us out (evil).

They worship in vain, teaching as doctrines the commandments of men. math 15:9

Conformity to insanity, sadism and verbal abuse of the left: snap back or nature wipes you out instead.

The democratic party has never been so upset since the Republicans outlawed slavery. Alex Jones

LEFT HATES OUR TRADITIONS AND CUSTOMS
Popularity does not determine truth--just the opposite.

The left wants to destroy our constitution, traditions/customs. They want us busted, or to be Muslims.

They parade like they're so superior: peas in a pod. Meanwhile they bash you a learned nerd as "odd".

The immoral Common Core stinks--turning sweet kids into sex pots and it's disgusting beyond belief.

Liberals breaking down into conniption fits over devastating defeat when they thought they were elite.

Why do they love disorder and collapse? Because they're the devil, absolute evil: learn the facts.

Thanksgiving saw families fighting over politics: it happens when you're frantic and they're thick as bricks.

ADAPTING TO A NARCISSIST RAT

Our dinner guest was so self-discrediting but she may not see it for several years, God be willing.

What a moral vanity trip she was on! Virtue signaling while being a moron incapable of polite conversation.

She discredited herself so thoroughly and even got drunk over it. Wow, universities: you're filled with it!

Don't you understand, he has to play the game with cards held close, ok? Their ego blinds them to the fake.

Obama's Whitehouse always sympathized with the killers, like thugs were his only emotional pillars.

You have to learn to stay apart from the mess: the church is full of ravenous wolves the bible confessed.

Everything in life—socially, emotionally, financially--tries to wear us down but with God, the crown.

THE DOUBLEMINDED ARE UNREWARDED

He won't receive a thing from the Lord bcuz he's double minded and unstable in all his ways.

The more they smear him the more I made the right decision cuz they're the problem/not solution.

The easily offended: easily manipulated and will always do crazy things to be accepted, never admitting it.

They don't feel we're in danger cuz they don't get the news--only state brainwashing, without a clue.

Why America's on the wane: Left wing policies brought staggering indebtedness impossible to maintain.

Now we really see who's dumb enough to go along with the herd. It lends discernment, a great barometer.

ADAPTING TO A NARCISSIST RAT

Soon we'll be rid of the filthy, debauched and sex-centered public schools and common core making whores.

I've been there, recall Vietnam? We were self-righteously angry too, but this new thing seems a scam.

Obama's "Medal of Freedom" was given out like lollipops to all his leftist friends/supporters though dumb.

Clinton and Podesta see it as a war and in war people do get killed: no big thing blood and gore.

TV is only good for old movies. Modern movies reflect liberalism since the sixties: cheap, dirty and cheesy.

CRY BABIES/DUMMIES DON'T KNOW HISTORY

Cry babies and dummies don't know history: Immoral, debauched, tainted, brainwashed, immature, lazy.

The freedom that creates so many fantastic opportunities is hated by the left and the globalists.

They bought into the false paradigm 8 years ago, delusionally thinking they were winners by condoning sinners.

They are the racists: All the KKK (krazy kollege kids) see is skin color and it's very serious with these brawlers.

I think you're so shallow you liked him for his looks and style. He was "cool" so you didn't see the hostile/vile.

Nothing tastes so delicious as vindication, more than riches. It is them not us who were the evil witches.

We went through too darn much to just sweep it under the couch, calling us arrogant fascists and grouch.

They act so superior, saying "what you said was so disturbing" as if you're bad not those heartless cads.

ADAPTING TO A NARCISSIST RAT

Trump's transfer of power to the states will be transformational and that will appeal to the least rational.

They perverted our will and our kids. They made us accept the unacceptable so we self-medicated/lost our lids.

Liberals are indecent trash. If there's any doubt lets discuss each point and you'll see they're scum/out for cash.

Trump will face the ridicule of treachery if he doesn't put Clinton misdeeds before a grand jury.

Don't be afraid, we're going to bring your country back. Donald Trump

HIX POLITIX UPDATES

The democrats want a permanent underclass.

Germany, compensating Nazi guilt, tells white citizens to prepare for demographic change/to be overrun.

Conservatives are just like everyone was in the 50's-60's before the hippies/feminist revolutionaries.

Tolerance and indulgence taken to absurd extremes is actually cruelty, brainwashing, being mean.

The people of Seattle are being asked to test out a theory that if police go away the crime goes away.

Outcomes: They want social justice not criminal justice and that's the beginning of the end like a holocaust.

Symptoms of addiction, mental illness or poverty are now LEGAL DEFENSES for crimes--"I was broke".

Assaults, harassment, trespass, breakins: crimes nullified cuz it's legal if you are a poor/crazy/addict.

People are convinced to do anything by shifting focus from the individual to the "good of the group".

ADAPTING TO A NARCISSIST RAT

That shift in focus from Christian/Americana individualism to the "good of the people" is entirely evil.

It's what YOU want not what's good for the others. Don't ever submerge yourself under the collective.

Would you talk out loud in a movie theater? Course not so please shut up when it's just me trying to hear.

The racist globalists are trying to kill off all the minorities "so cursed" by giving them the vaccines first.

HOMESTEAD UPDATES

Aristocratic Neatness is pure class and it's what I want in every room and drawer, the kitchen first.

No one takes GLYCATION as their major diet matrix but I see it as central--delete signs of aging now.

Ha Ha: Coconut products are sky-high glycation, along with avocados, dairy, nuts, all oils, animal.

Look at food as INFORMATION which tells genes and DNA to turn off or on, hormones too, digestion.

How can we so desperately need meat, when billions live on rice and are much thinner/quicker please?

I don't want you to be gone in your sixties, I picture you being wheeled into ER from your meat feasts.

Millions die in their sleep but it's really from CHOKING and so I say: Just Skip Dinner and wake up lively.

My one addiction is Cheetos--so I may take a couple, so what. It's just the delicious taste I love.

Go ahead and eat your meat, it is none of my business anyway. I'd just hate to lose you suddenly.

ADAPTING TO A NARCISSIST RAT

Billions of people live on rice. They're thin and. quick, we're fat and sick so just think about this.

If you don't like your cherry smoothie add plant-based nonfat yogurt and lotsa dates in the blend.

DAM RATS

Smears and Virtue Signaling

ALTERCATIONS BEFORE TOTAL SUCCESS
SEE BEHIND MASKS!
DECOMPENSATIONS: WIFE OF ALCOHOLIC
PURSUE YOUR LIFE'S WORK AMIDST CHAOS
MENTAL ILLNESS IS JUST MAL-ADAPTATION
SATAN WANTS YOU CONFUSED
STAYING ORDERLY AMIDST CHAOS
BE NICE: BRING OUT THEIR BEST
CHAOS VS. SOLITUDE
NEED FOR *PRIVACY*, NOT SOCIAL!
REMAIN INACCESSIBLE TO BE KING
SOCIAL GATHERINGS ARE SICKENING AND BORING
WHOOPI AND THE OPPRESSION HIERARCHY PYRAMID
DOWNPLAYING MASS MURDER
APATHY VS. AWARENESS OF ENORMITY
WAS SLAVERY RACISM OR INHUMANITY?
JUST A BUNCHA WHITES FIGHTING
A COVER FOR HOLOCAUST DENIERS
THEY DON'T FORGIVE US FOR THE SLIGHTEST

DAM RATS

Smears and Virtue Signaling

TAKING LEISURE IS A GENIUS MARKER
PREPARE FOR SYSTEM INVERSION (ENANTIODROMIA)!
CLARITY AND COMPLETION
GET YOUR PRIORITIES RIGHT
DISINHERIT THE JERKS!
WOMEN CAJOLED TO ABORT AND DIVORCE!
SMILE OR YOU'RE MEAN, THE MEAN DON'T SMILE
FAKE GLOBALIST MEDIA IS HATED (CNN +)
HILLARY WOULDA BEEN THE END
TARGETING GROUPS IS TERRORISM
LIBERALS CRAZY OVER WORDS NOT ACTIONS
GENERAL PUBLIC IS DUMB AS HELL
CAN'T FIGHT FOR LIBERTY IF NEEDING APPROVAL
ABSURD DEMANDS OF SOCIAL JUSTICE WARRIORS
LEFT-RIGHT DIVISION IS EXPLODING
LIBERALS ARE A PATHOLOGICAL HEX
AN ENTIRE GENERATION LOST HOW TO THINK
GENDER PRONOUNS AND OTHER DUMBS
FEMALE COMMIES IN YOUR OWN FAMILY?

CONSERVATIVE / LIBERAL

Borders / Open Borders
Anti-Crime / Coddles criminals
Religion / Aethism "Gaya"
Family / Anti-Family
Two genders / Multi-genders
Tough on enemies / Appease enemies
Love America / Hate America
Nationalism / Globalism
Anti-abortion / Abort without restrictions
Racial pride / Globalism: "all one"
State owns children. / Parents own em
Sex education / Parents determine
Green New Deal / It's all bull

MOST IMPORTANT DIFFERENCE
vision of future utopia / sees things as they ARE

DAM RATS
Smears and Virtue Signaling

Systems Theory: how the system creates/maintains pathology in the one: the identified patient seen as scum.

The lower (the past, first) is holding you down. Let it go, it was just a scaffold while you grew a crown.

How the tables have turned! What was up is now down and the down is on top and revered.

It's New Age to be positive: thinking everything's ok when it isn't. That's not loving, you're really missing it.

Transcend and forget those who wanted you locked up/dead. Turn your attention now to loving your pets.

To get to success divide from old systems keeping you down. This is a necessity before receiving the crown.

Fake-friendly: You're "family" until you don't buy it (won't deny it) then you're ostracized, believe it.

If you fit you're illegit. If you don't it may mean you're God's kid.

ALTERCATIONS BEFORE TOTAL SUCCESS

There's always an altercation right before becoming famous and rich. It's like the test, rejecting the witch.

Picture the bad past as a dirty ugly swamp filled with mosquitoes: this mental picture of foes says so!

Their demeaning influence is felt on a cellular level but often denied. You're sick inside, eat/drink to quiet the tide.

DAM RATS

LIVE TO SEASONS OF THE DAY

Live your own life according to the seasons of the day, with good routines and utter decency.

Studies show they burned the witches outa jealousy. What does this tell us about treachery?

If you don't act right you come under other's control and you won't like that loss of freedom girl.

WE WANT: Family, country, God, freedom, low taxes and regulations, borders against invasion.

Liberals want whatever fits their utopian vision, a worked out cosmology: "we are one".

We want family, country, God, freedom, low taxes and regulations and borders against invasion.

Yes Sir, as long as you hold my head above water and take an interest in our homestead here.

SO YOU CAUSED A RIPPLE

You caused a ripple and it went thru grapevine and you felt exposed/called swine, I know, aye.

That land you bought is not to fill up but a **BUFFER ZONE** between you and the mob.

Nothing's more important than privacy otherwise I get so nervous I wanna die/honest/no lie.

The queen has perfect privacy the inferior socials do not. They know nothing of cerebrotonics.

In the Cinderella Syndrome it's always two against one. This triangulation is strangulation hon'.

DAM RATS

STIGMA: They perceive you thru an archetype, not the real you. That's why to be extra careful.

Being different/rejected from the herd brings shame in wolves who die. Honor unique peculiarity.

There's also hereditary shame--cuz they want you to feel that way so you feel bad/do it again.

ALCOHOL AND ANGELS

The thing about alcohol is you never know. Sometimes it works/sometimes it pegs you down low.

The devil WAITS. At the most inopportune & crucial time he can take over if you're drinkin' ok.

It's a tragic habit. You always want more, you're nursing a hangover, each day you start earlier.

It will happen when God deems it to and not one second before. Relax, He's got you covered.

Shane: I guess I should thank you cuz you taught me to trust no one. You were the last one son.

I pray for the realization of the Creative Act on earth when all of a sudden you come first.

You can be happy and optimistic about you in your own stream but not the tragic liberal lunatics.

They'll say my God we killed [be-smudged, smeared, murdered the rep of] a genius and saint!

SHAME

We gotta deal with SHAME inherited or not. It will weigh you down, an obstruction & knot.

DAM RATS

Repent of whatcha got to then go on, Jesus doesn't want you sad or reliving that wrong.

SHAME is usually cuz you're different from the pack not a justified feeling like you're bad.

You already have winning energy, blocked by obstruction--food, habits, people: debris.

The mean and cruel method of hanging by cranes isn't sudden but drawn out suffocation.

Stop remorsing over when the devil had control of the vessel because it wasn't you AT ALL.

SHAME IS A BURDEN

Drop shame or it burdens, obstructs and destroys. It weighs us down with thoughts of yesterday.

Shame came from not fitting the tribe then to correct it taking the wrong path of joining groups.

Your work will no longer be drudgery and every moment a shimmering light in your memory.

Get married then every meal's a banquet and every day's a holiday and get a high wall ok.

If it's of God it will work out perfectly as it always has and if not well you wouldn't want it sis.

Jesus doesn't want us to be afraid of anything including our own past. No guilt we let it go at last.

As you view movie think of driving AWAY from past problems thinking only good memories.

You don't threaten murder and get away with it. Evil always goes too far/does itself in.

DAM RATS

CRIME AND HIX POLITIX

Education is a weapon whose effect depends on who holds it and at who it is aimed. Stalin

Public schools are a weapon straight out of the communist playbook--the "free collage" hook.

They see our apathy as a license to steal galore. Picasso: Hunter's paintings are worth more?

Washington D. C. is now a business model for many to get rich--mainly corporate and BIG TECH.

Corporatocracy: All political entities like education controlled by corporate interests exclusively.

Biden's the biggest hater while our worker's wages turn to dust by inflation and foreign invaders.

Biden hates American workers as it all goes to hell and even so he refuses to build more wall.

But we can't criticize it cuz they're in bed with the media and tech giants who will cancel us.

PASSIVE COMPLIANCE IS PERMISSION

Passive compliance to corruption is always interpreted as permission as it finally rots the system.

Brainwash by corps until a rotted system finally keels over cuz no one takes it seriously anymore.

Trump called out rotting swamp for what they are but in era of hyper-normalization this is barred.

In the globalist worldview you can't call em invaders or foreign workers but World Citizens sir.

DAM RATS

Trump called out FOX for going left but now Tucker, Laura et. al. are fueling our rise instead.

The patriotic godly right is rising up again in this century so hold up your chin and repent of sin.

The false church thinks universality is godly, the "we are one" fallacy but we're different see.

NO BORDERS IS UNGODLY

It is **NOT** godly to let em all in. It's of the devil to invade the privacy of your own people, it is treason.

It's **NOT** godly to let em all in. It's evil to care more for outsiders than insiders--it is **TREASON**.

Trumpism was the **PEOPLE** vs. the rotting political class which, just like Soviet Russia, will collapse.

How many kids refuse to resuscitate old parents when they look forward to a big allowance?

This is just the latest example of the whole Hypocrisy Industry leading our climate policies.

They tell us we must be poorer in order to save the planet while they accumulate billions for it.

WORK THOUGHTS

The dense ask me to explain, I go to much trouble writing it out again, then they don't mention it.

He's not trained to write code for designers but force the designer thru his program: e.g.word press.

They all say they can write code but give em your design and they're floored, the answer is no.

DAM RATS

THOUGH DRIVEN INSANE

Liberals just talk like they're superior and you're a dunce. Only the strongest can overcome this.

Tho' a liberal sister drove me insane it was still my fault for falling into my bag of devices for coping.

I said and did things that were NOT ME. But because I was weak thru sin up comes another entity.

I think I'm ok today, totally mature--having been tested under fire in extremely bad conditions, dire.

Getting all their flying monkeys against you is the same as saying all they do is gossip to their friends.

The long distance relationship stuff can turn off or on the other hand it can get more hot.

"Gotta get him back, life could go downhill from here but he's looking greasy maybe better an affair."

Due to age you're seen you as weak, obsolete, ineffectual, a joke, outmoded so push back and show em.

THE NEW SELF BASED ON ROUTINES

I didn't have a self so made a new one based on my routines, homelife, pets and work habits.

I didn't have a self so made a NEW one based on routines, homelife, pets, studied worldview, work habits.

I made a NEW self based on what God designed before birth but I had to repent to find that groove.

Due to age you're seen you as weak/obsolete/ineffectual, a joke/outmoded so gird up and push back.

DAM RATS

The long-distance relationship can peter out as you give up or get more hot as you're thinking about.

I know there's telepathy between you and me--its obvious you see--and it makes me very happy.

After a lifetime of work I stand on the pinnacle of world success, exhausted but filled with bliss.

I'm filled with the knowledge of you and me but it's gonna remain our secret--that's all it can ever be.

Great scholars in history had love notes all thru their works of genius until the Lord frees us.

The greater the intellectual life the deeper the love but with things like alcoholism the worse the strife.

SPOUSE IS YOUR FENCE

There's a social vs. spiritual world. People worship people before God so Satan's having a ball.

You think you can talk to somebody, a good ol' guy--but he turns out cold, missing, inconsistent, a spy.

I don't care what you look like if you hold me at night, do the manly stuff, give me privacy, enjoy it all.

What's the manly stuff? Protection & provision though I'm sure together we'd succeed far higher.

An intellectual can't take contradiction so with the Dunning-Kruger effect it's an **EXPLOSION**.

Say what you want about Ray he was a **FENCE** and that's enough for me--to get you blocked/to be free.

So that's all I gotta say today hon', enjoy your day under the sun, I've got my music, musing and fun.

DAM RATS

I'm always alone. Can you stand being with one so introverted, otherworldly--refusing to be a clone?

That was your problem your entire life: YOU taking on THEIR reality about YOU--quit this/stay high.

Your highest test: maintain YOUR reality amongst gainsayers, detractors and enemies.

Remove this guy: now you'll have Found Time and wonder why you waited so long to fly.

Most productive/evocative thing I do: looking out the window. Second most: music with the view.

I thank God for the talents He has given me. They're sharp now having evolved thru a lifetime.

Stop kidding yourself, he's not there for you. He's not interested and has many better things to do.

There's a designation called Moral Insanity and I guess that was me or was I just sick you think?

I TAKE EVERYTHING PERSONALLY

Better be careful with me cuz I take everything personally. EVERYTHING is run through my mind buddy.

Few politicians turn down million dollar tips to cast a vote/change route but that's what it's all about.

Politicians can't do it: Turning down a million bucks to do/say this or that--can you imagine it?

Substitute intrusive thoughts from when vulnerable and unprotected cuz you're missing the present.

Traditionally women are turned on by a man who supports them--not bring down their house, how dumb.

DAM RATS

Proper perspective: The only hell I experienced was you dropping over, after all I didn't go to war.

The only cage I ever experienced was a relationship with you, after all I didn't go to prison with felons.

Just cuz a sentence isn't given immediately they think they're Scot free but hell no, they'll see.

These traitors will be sought out and brought to justice. We've had enough frustration with all this.

Expect enemy to flourish like the olive tree but soon after mowed down like old dry grass, you'll see.

His refusal to respond like any decent person is due to guilt as God pours coals on his head now son.

NO I'M NOT COMING BACK

No I'm not going back to you. You were only a lesson and I don't repeat the same, I progress quickly on.

Though just a brief email response instinctively I never wanted to connect again: that's a WIN.

There's few women who haven't been molested. Now the boys too, all have seen treachery/rejection.

Gee, the media stayed blind to voter fraud just as they did Biden's laptop but how they mock Trump.

Liberal brings his friends who rob me. He begs for drug money then acts like he's gonna hit me.

If someone's doing an act when you give em an edge they'll over-reach showing them as a leech.

CLARITY IS HEALTHY FEAR OF PEOPLE

DAM RATS

Clarity brings healthy fear of the human race. They're all filthy rags with wicked hearts the Bible says.

You incurred disaster on me in a small town. It was easy for you being social and me not yet renowned.

You incurred opprobrium on me in a small town--it's easy for a ruthless gossip with your social wisdom.

You knew everyone's name in a small town while I knew no one. I had a husband but he was drunken.

I know how women compete and play the game. They get the others against you, the odd girl out dame.

JUSTICE NECESSARY FOR RELIEF

JUSTICE is necessary for the relief of the saints. We've held it in for too long while they got away.

With a narcissist like him you ONLY have control by going no-contact, then you forget all about it.

JUSTICE is happening now with mass arrests and OH what a feeling after a decade suppressing.

Even your bothersome peculiarities God eventually wove into a good pattern like turning water into wine.

It's not multiple personality, it's maximum elasticity. I can be anything you or I want me to be honey.

You'll need a very peculiar woman to fit your needs. Am I that woman sweetie? If so it's destiny.

I learned alot about German women adapting to my mother and sisters and they were meanies.

COLLAPSED FEMALE NARCISSIST

DAM RATS

Theory Building: As the formula illuminates some things take precedence/some things fade to the back.

Female narcissism is a house built on stilts. She's high on the hog till a wind blows It down then she's nuts.

Tho' the collapsed female narcissist looks pitiful and powerless she's still a barracuda/tigress.

The aging collapsed female narcissist has nothing more to lose so have caution because it gets cruel.

Stop coming to my home. i'm having a ball and don't want you around--I wanna go solo so now GO.

The perfect setup for the aging female narcissist: we live in two houses for protection and privacy both.

Everything's about me but can't you see? I had to centralize power in defense against treachery.

In this dire hour I have learned something so special and empowering: more alone, more power.

BEING ALONE IS PURE POWER

In healthy generations being alone may have been less empowering but not now, it's WAY more.

Historically presidents showed tremendous power in extraordinary times: Lincoln/Churchill/Trump.

Democrats are a party of marginalized groups, tech and financial bigwigs and intellectual socialists.

Yes it seems I'm allergic to everything but finding these limitations increases your power don't you see?

Every time narcissist doesn't get what he wants he becomes inconsolably angry--a dangerous rut.

DAM RATS

Always remember: the narcissists will devalue you while getting supply from you--they're disloyal.

Always remember: the narcissists will devalue you while getting supply from you cuz they're disloyal.

When you cut him off to attend to your needs--like privacy--that's when he really rages, you'll see.

Trauma-bonding, abuse-amnesia and feeling lonely can lead one to make bad, VERY bad decisions.

SUPPRESSED ANGER

You must recognize your justifiable anger cuz it's physical effects are devastating and not going away.

Suppressed anger creates: clenched jaw, gut aches, acid reflux and a racing heart all over the place.

The Silent Treatment is the female narcissist's favorite control tactic, going on for months in fact.

Her other two powerful manipulations are guilt trips and withholding affection which works like magic.

If you don't like it don't go to my channel, page, website or anything. That's the whole point: autonomy.

When in doubt it's best taking the high road. You know which one that is, it means you're alone.

GO NO-CONTACT WITH THE WHOLE TRIBE

Will you have to go no-contact with your whole tribe? Yes, every last one cuz it's a SYSTEM, aye?

The original perpetrators may not be alive but the SYSTEM persists and it's all against you and I.

DAM RATS

It's the black sheep in mind--a groove made by years of eery misjudgment that's now been encrypted.

Where did misjudgment come from? The same person who killed her husband with the same jargon.

The same feminist slogan-driven misjudgment killed her husband then was turned on me ma'am.

He was friendly 'til he talked to his wife then came back angry, mad, dismissively turning the knife.

WOMEN ARE INFERIOR THINKERS

Women are such inferior thinkers they're still for Hillary and Bernie but in the family it's a tragedy.

Women are such inferior thinkers they still like the fake Indian Pocahontas-- what's her name, Warren?

We all have inferior thinking females in our family who are dragging us down into something very shady.

I couldn't stand her the minute she entered the family. Who did she think she was acting so haughty?

Her inferior thinking bamboozled her nice husband then like a cancer it took over the whole system.

She acted so superior in her inferior "knowledge" which was mere slogans spouted from college.

And thus we have the dumbing down of the whole family cuz the STEM of true wisdom was gone forever.

The STEM of Christianity was gone forever: what was left were evil offshoots so letting go was easier.

I avoided the youth and stuck with the oldsters of the tribe then cut it all loose when they died.

DAM RATS

There's nothing more sickening and dark then going to a family dinner with liberals who think like that.

We've only one life to live and when the good ones are gone you gotta dismiss all this and get on with it.

All they did was talk liberal BS in my face and acted so superior while doing it the dirty phony twits.

If you need to get out this is NOT your family--they are aliens/bottom-feeders from below believe me.

I saw "family" like religious orthodoxy then saw it was fantasy--Jesus came with a sword you see.

They hang together like peas in a pod. A genius like her can't take that as they mock and call her odd.

I'm suffering 35 years later and the events are more lucid than ever. PTSD just isn't fair.

WHEN THE SYSTEM GOES DARK

When a system goes dark like that you hate every single one of em. They're a blob and you're that ONE.

Being alone is pure potent power while being with you is contamination and boredom.

When a Christian is born again he becomes a whole new kind of person separate from the original one.

If you think there's gonna be a perfect fit you've much to learn cuz systems will band together and hit.

When the last of the stem was dead I was terrified of what was left, a mob of unrecognizable leftists.

And for this reason, marriage is substitutionary. It wipes out the lower/other, all the original clutter.

DAM RATS

Liberals are pawns for globalists but are killed first. That's how all revolutions work by such jerks.

MARRIAGE SOLVES PEOPLE PROBLEMS

As soon as I got married ALL problems stopped--they were PEOPLE PROBLEMS. What a revelation.

Something happened to brain at a young age having to do with that cage and I got crazy, then a sage.

Just the thought someone would listen to me and care what I think was too good to be true you see.

I don't care what you look like as long as you hold me at night. People age at different rates, so what.

Your diet worked at first cuz everything does work at first even their drugs then there's hell longterm.

It's a thing in our heads, a definite division. Just that mere recognition saved many lady vegans.

The meat-eating thing will be a crossroads in any relationship with a vegan, count on it.

They think it's about vanity rather than a fatal mental illness so they think nothing of rejecting us.

It's about SUGAR--glucose--not whether it's organic juicy fruit tho' of course we choose a high source.

I don't know where this is coming from or why God chose me as a vessel for his Great Work and Wonder.

The spontaneous interview leaves too much room for imperfection and could come off wrong.

Less pictures, more recognizable don't you see that you imbecile flooding us with this stuff I throw.

DAM RATS

They're so jealous of you it eats them alive. Their ego can't take it so they hate you/feels like a knife.

Block em all. Don't give em a chance to hurt you again, entangling you in an envy-ridden lion's den.

Never throw your pearls before swine lest you be trampled by them. They don't just snub, they ruin.

I went from the worst setup to loving support and life's now a crack up--that's marriage, it makes it all up.

You can't make people good by hanging with em. They'll just drag you down and remember it's subtle/no fun.

Determine to be exceptional, hard-working, inventive and good. Not superficial/carnal with heart of wood.

SEE BEHIND MASKS!

Must see what people are really like behind the mask. Don't feel mean--it's an incredibly beneficial task.

Just cuz you forgive one doesn't mean you gotta have em around. Forgive but don't forget and stay crowned.

Emotional Illness: a trauma happens they can't deal with so they eat/drink in excess to cover the mess.

Sexy trendies: Show me your subscription list and I'll know your intelligence--just superficialities.

Genius comes from God through us--if clear of obstructions called "sin" which plagues/makes us joyless.

You became the worst of the lot cuz hypersensitivity made you most susceptible and pliable to devils.

Sin is a device to avoid anxiety. Make gold on the habit and you shoot up to world renowned victory.

DAM RATS

Big problem of saints is excruciating remorse over past sins, despite knowing it was all erased by Him.

The repentant saints feel remorse for they have a stinging conscience while everyone else is dense.

Retirement is when you can so what you want, finally--and to hell with the rest, the common tragedy.

Though you may hate their guts be cordial and gracious always/don't stop.

Just cuz you forgive one doesn't mean you must them around. Forgive but don't forget and stay crowned.

Leave the lower (apathetic, pathetic, a wreck) for the higher (aesthetic, energetic, magnetic and poetic).

DECOMPENSATIONS: WIFE OF ALCOHOLIC

Wife of the alcoholic complains of his drinking for decades but it's when he stops that she goes crazy.

Never has society been so uncivil. Even friends will turn and swivel. They've all gone mad/are so fickle.

I will never phone with her. She subtly, jealously snipes and can't resist the temptation to slur.

The sly are subtle--don't forget that now! Never question your instincts when dealing with the low.

Sounds like a misanthrope but it's reality folks

It's just like the bible shows us. The world has wicked and righteous: two groups and that's why we fuss.

Cuz I love animals God gave me a house, fenced yard, dog door and joy galore--who would want more.

Not all mothers come from God--some come from the devil. What will you do then? Get out on the double.

DAM RATS

If you hang with hogs you'll get dirty like em: just cogs in the wheel (no power) so watch who you befriend.

You can sink cuza who your friends are--you stink as you mal-adapt/fall so far. Stay in the pink: clear the air.

If you're talented but your parents/spouses are hicks you must respect them anyway or it acts as a hex.

Detractors: Whoever I met they would call before, planting evil seeds. They wanted me powerless/on my knees.

Once you get your act together escape into a romantic/magical life. If feeling out of synchrony, just be nice.

PURSUE YOUR LIFE'S WORK AMIDST CHAOS

You've worked all your life to get to this point. Now your time has finally come and God will anoint.

Evergreen: Like best films or wine you get better, more archetypal and stronger influence with time.

More millionaires created in depression than any time in history. They didn't see misery but opportunity.

Strong minds can maintain a thought. The rest are just taken off--everything you taught em was for naught.

Their homes are built on sand. That's their mind--ever with the party line while you always question.

They agree wholeheartedly then are swept away with the first opportunity. Give up on them, see eternity!

Just act like you're an actress and your job is to be beautiful and you'll have every day completely full.

Every theory they come up with is self-justification for perversion and they don't seek higher for wisdom.

DAM RATS

From worst to best, from most inferior to most superior--I'm delirious, yes sir

Forget your crazy siblings, your mother and father loved you: apple of their eye/thought you were cute!

It's not the end: you're at your top! Remember that when you feel like a wet mop due to youthist snobs.

MENTAL ILLNESS IS JUST MAL-ADAPTATION

Don't blame yourself for mental illness that happened to you, the only way you could adapt for you.

Poets are higher than writers. They're actually scientific discoverers that come around every 40 years.

Through diet, solitude, athletics I escaped everything my mother had to go through due to genetics and frenetics.

How to control your frenetic new puppy: Put on nice music, he'll calm down (like a miracle) and stay happy.

It's as if the low rung/past morphs into something you don't recognize or never knew. Life stages renew!

Your gut feels it first. That's the solar plexus sensing disequilibrium with the environment, the worst.

They disdain your unique (cute) differences. You're not like them, the (imagined) prince/princesses.

Rather than a grand piano clogging my living room I like chillout heavy on the bass and for dogs lotsa space.

As good as it gets: A cozy cabin feeling such comfort on a rainy day with good books and pets.

I feel very vulnerable living in Borrego or California in general. I'll head to the center for life potential.

DAM RATS

You get to a point where it's so murky you can't proceed without blind faith but God's there always.

A point of critical mass has been reached. I'm blinded by confusion so it's God I've beseeched.

The only answer to total confusion is blind faith. God reveals the simple answer (that's grace).

Maybe confusion and chaos is good since it leads us to the clarity, order and simplicity of God.

SATAN WANTS YOU CONFUSED

Satan wants us to be confused--he's the author of it! Turn to God, simple as a child, He'll solve it.

I'm in a very dark place: chaos--knowing nothing--but at least I'm not in the past called disgrace.

Dogs: man's best friends. Love them, but the most important thing is: you're with them to the end.

With a low threshold to pain I'm more dependent on God's grace than ever but He is so clever!

You decide your path, or take what you're served. The latter I will not, I choose my lot.

You reach a point where you're fed up to "here"--you've had it! No more being derailed--just stop it.

Don't let em bog you down in details. That's what you pay them for: you're an artist so stay simple.

We're a dying breed--dinosaurs--cuz people can't even reason anymore, so show your elderhood, soar.

Give up on them, you must! Just expand your own talents--what you're on earth for--or rust.

DAM RATS

STAYING ORDERLY AMIDST CHAOS

I can see why you're goin down--lost in detail. Rise up to a bird's eye view of why you always fail.

Record it somewhere and sort it out later. Make sure you write it all down to later be an activator.

Introverts are drained by small talk cuz it feels fake and meaningless—now that's a sign of genius.

God's going to get the creeps that hurt animals and you should too. Show them rightness, be the proof.

Husband: Where he really shines is where I direct his mind. He focuses and solves everything so fine.

He takes care of details so I can do my thing--and I sweep, dust and order so he feels like a king.

I gotta be creative and clear--not taking psych-drugs/feeling like I'm at the bottom of a pit in despair.

Any woman borrowing masculine identity has a rough edge, see? Not tender and sweet as she could be.

All that matters is creativity, so make your life about that by eliminating the news and empty chats.

Sensitivity to chemicals, light and pain is very isolating but you learn who your friends are vs. enemies.

Don't nag, be what you say he should be. Be an examplar defined by repentance and consistency.

Sensitivity to chemicals and pain go together--the immune system is so busy it can't handle more.

No matter what they say, God can turn judgment away though we sinned every day.

DAM RATS

You can't successfully smoke it without coughing. That is the whole problem and I'm not kidding.

BE NICE: BRING OUT THEIR BEST

Unless in deep sin, don't judge your mate. Look past it all, to who they can be if you're nice/not irate.

When his old tactic fails he stops the behavior but then uses another tactic, oh well Pavlov's bell.

The spirit of control comes a hundred fold in various poses like being cold but resist it, and be bold.

Humble yourselves to God, not man. Cut out being used and calling it humility cuz God hates that.

The spirit of control wants to be God in your life: laying down before a steamroller creates strife.

If there are still people/areas holding us back, then they are determining how far we can go, in fact.

The world must be seen as dung or we're always being re-anchored, tied to the tired and down.

The Lord calls us out of bondage. That's outa the world and it's ways into His kingdom = fantastic!

If the spirit of control loses power with you he doesn't recognize you. It's principalities and powers fool.

Since the spirit of control works through our past, we must drop it at last.

CHAOS VS. SOLITUDE

Your most productive time is looking out the window or puttering.

One fears fame though it's the name of the game. You've done the work now show the world the Dame.

DAM RATS

My problem was seeing people as important and apathy towards God--and thus I felt minimized and odd.

We were told our worth was dependent on how social we were in the eyes of the herd--were we preferred?

Fame and fortune will change everything so just keep truckin'--no need for fakin'--look beyond your situation.

We do best in our own stream at our own speed: mine was introverted reclusion with no social needs.

We come in alone, we die alone so don't hang on/avoid the throng.

They're all on probation with me.

Control your life (locked gate) or too many surprises (mean fate).

Need for privacy is not against people but knowing I'm in control/alone or it's a mental hazard (de-throned).

If you only get privacy when they're willing to give it to you then they're masters of your fate not you.

Privacy is an inalienable right and constitutional. Everyone knows a slave's business, that's low and it's bull.

NEED FOR *PRIVACY*, NOT SOCIAL!

Need for privacy offends women who are social. They haven't a clue cuz just to live they need other people.

Just cuz the little people can't understand it doesn't mean you're wrong or should give up on it, man.

Interruptions and invasions are a mental hazard cuz you never know when you're free (can be alone), see?

Give your social neighbor the key to your gate for emergencies only and soon he'll abuse this privilege.

DAM RATS

Professional man has secretary to act as a screen. What if anyone could invade him--wouldn't happen, see?

If they have a key they're in control when they see you--not you--and that's the basis for vacuity/being blue.

Forget em. Hate to say it but time is getting late. Get your trusted network together or expect bad fate.

People don't get to see you just cuz they want to. You determine that but the truly mature are few.

If people can see you though you don't want to, you're their slave. Get class--exclude, choose destiny, be a rave.

Communist (public) schools forced us to be social. Privacy is a sin to them so they force themselves on y'all.

REMAIN INACCESSIBLE TO BE KING

They want what they want (to see you) so use excuses to circumvent your requirements/will pay for this.

Group comes first in the communist schools: loyalty transcends autonomy (it's hell for the genius, really).

Control your life (locked gate) or too many surprises (mean fate).

These people are invasive (sneaky) and officious (nosy). Withdraw from social tyranny and take back the key.

You're not living if can't get privacy in your own home though at times they give you "space" (throw you a bone).

They force you to lay down the law constantly. They just don't get it and will impose themselves 'til you're silly.

Hillary is communist: stronger together, village raises child, female community: stormy weather.

DAM RATS

Caveat: They aren't gonna let you get what you want (privacy) cuz it's a loss for them/they will get back.

Creative people in the right-brain can't live in time. Such schedules wreck their art and ruin their prime.

A young male may do anything to be with an older woman with money. You must recognize/stop it honey.

The puppy's trying to find his parameters of do's/dont's and all you're doing is yelling at him—no, love him.

SOCIAL GATHERINGS ARE SICKENING AND BORING

The reason social gatherings are sickening: there's always something.

It took years to learn my lines. What I could take/couldn't, need for borders, hating grossness/loving refined.

I gotta do what I do. I can't stop telling what they're up to. It's about maintaining home/staying cute.

A true lady has class, elegance, gentleness, assiduity, tenderness, ability to love and respect for her husband.

Even if I didn't love you we'd still be married cuz it's about God and His covenants—to the herd this is odd.

Forward: at the front, ahead, advanced, onward, prompt, ready, bold, presumptuous, futuristic.

I want things neat all the time or as a cerebrotonic I feel disorderly and crazy.

The good thing about money is you can do your own thing/not be beholden to anybody.

The magic carpet ride is: being rid of the past. This psychic opening is a blast.

The past has abnormal control over the present so just learn what you must and good riddance.

DAM RATS

"It just is": So long as divorce is an option you're always doubting and looking around.

Nothing works but Jesus. That's why you're unhappy and keep tryin' to please us.

I wanna look at the view. I wanna see weather and take in all of God's nature too.

Obstructions of people, habit and food muck up the works--make us indifferent or jerks.

My insecurities compel constant improvement and that's why I work every single moment.

TAKING LEISURE IS A GENIUS MARKER

I can't take any more, just listen to music. It's horrible what's happening but God said praise it.

Let no one tell you how to do it. Get the gist then on it put your twist and that's the perfect fix.

Poet: political-psychological pundit I guess you'd call it and that's cuz I know it having gone through it.

I don't care what anyone says. This is true maturity: it's the True Self and God who created it, always.

I'll get the main headlines but all these details I'll let go cuz life is a pie and it's my groove I'll refine.

I've come to just appreciate what I see out my window. In situ: just my own situation, ya know.

I don't care about the movie I just want it to evoke thought in me. I stop it often to write and think.

She doesn't inspire me to wear a bikini, just to be the best I can be and that also means physically.

DAM RATS

Hurray! You have the answer: Fast and pray. It's so easy/costs nothing as it saves the day.

So what if he's a cute kid--Satan uses the shy and sheepish. Don't judge by appearances, Paul admonishes.

If they don't come when they say nor put things back in place they're immature/still a baby face.

My bruised adult ego still won't let go but I'll pray about it and see if they are someone I should know.

Get past looks. For some that's all it took as they settle down to solid and stable life (no deception/strife).

Never trust people who stand you up. Even once is a no-brainer: a sign of disrespect/dumb schmucks.

PREPARE FOR SYSTEM INVERSION (ENANTIODROMIA)!

Now is the time for System Inversion (enantiodromia) as the bottom becomes the top--oh my!

You had yours, now it's my time to shine. We'll all disappear but for now, seasons of cheer (no beer).

She always just escaped me, she was never there. Ended in a rest home and then she disappeared.

I honestly can't take it anymore. I've done my part now I just wanna explore my own inner journey with art galore.

Just remember the most important comes first. That's what gets attention and makes them read further.

The Creative Act is a baby you carry for decades then you finally give birth and it's recognized by the world.

Celebrate your success before it happens. Create the mood, man: happiness!

DAM RATS

Mom said just wear what I have on. Synchronicity not put-ons (be gone).

One never knows when he'll be done until that moment he's done. Albert Einstein

CLARITY AND COMPLETION

This is the last brick in the building: completion of the creative act. If you're willing, it's a whole new life in fact.

Few have opportunity to pursue their talents. Problems in their network or false ideas and they lose all chance.

Home: Obama and cronies aren't here and out there Donald will take care of it, our dear. Relax, not a tear.

All that matters is you love it. Doesn't matter what they think, if they like it or even if they hate all of it.

To an inner genius or the saints the outer world is loud, noisy, cacophonous, irritating and disorderly.

Don't get messed up with emotional entanglements and jealousy triangles from situations long ago.

You can be eclipsed by another human as an overshadowing influence: Spirit crushed, mind a dunce.

The sexes need each other. For example females have a problem with completion/need male vision.

A good marriage is 2 + 2 = 20,000. It's dynamite, the royal couple and it means wealth and elation.

You reach your peak and then you decline--so what? We all have a place in the sun at a certain date and time.

So much wasted time worrying when soon you will be dead. Why not make a mark instead--get out the lead.

Nothing fascinates like your own mind. You've forgotten that filling time.

DAM RATS

Intelligence, audacity, cleverness.

Make yourself "apt" to receive. Sit down, look out the window, believe.

Wow, I can leave the chaos and just float on Holy Spirit Ease, productive puttering with dear Lord Jesus.

Personally it's turning out to be a wonderful time. Everything's coming together beautifully as if divine.

First they ignore, then they laugh, then they fight you and then you win. Gandhi "The obstacle is the path."

Just cuz you have nothing to hide doesn't mean they can't set you up. We have reason to fear but look up.

GET YOUR PRIORITIES RIGHT

Substitute love for dead logs who couldn't care less for the eternal Jesus and forget the dying moths, the godless.

Love takes sacrifice but they're all about "getting my needs met". Sickening, truly. I worry about kids/pets.

Crippled in the free market because they don't know how to fail, reason, write, think or debate.

Helpless victims become vicious abusers. Greater the childhood trauma the greater the addiction.

We've had a dose of female logic in Pelosi, Watters, Clinton and the future is ruled by same warped vision.

Let no one tell you how to do it. You were born for it but needed to grow into it and that took ruin.

To be a success all you need is finish high school, be married before babies, get a job. Ben Shapiro

Marriage is a divine institution. Being alone's not good but joining forces makes life a celebration.

DAM RATS

If you're smart but with the wrong premise or principals you can reason your way to your own funeral.

I always loved the Lord but couldn't stand when church became a brick to carry not a lamp to guide/bored.

Sin is a device to deal with anxiety. It works for awhile then the serpent turns back to strike with insanity.

Don't tell me to go anywhere, it's flawed. It's boring, tedious or debauched and I just wanna be with God.

Disorder reflects mind. Clear minds can't stand it--they want clarity, beauty, order from chaos: the refined.

You're outa sorts from someone in your network. Cut em loose, that's the power of disengagement, it works.

DISINHERIT THE JERKS!

Heck, disinherit the jerks.

You must be mentally free to think, talk and write so get em out of your perception: no more silly P.C.!

Since I was a grasshopper in their eyes I became a grasshopper. I got strong and unswayable when I got older.

The saints show an unheard of level of courage in public. William James

Everyone knows clean order is superior to dirty disorder, or do they?

Music is everything to me. It makes me think, how to be more free.

Genius mistrusts words.

Christian women learn how not to hate the husband but love him, amen? Our tendency is to see their imperfections but that we must overcome.

Music changes everything instantly and I've learned to have it on constantly, happily

DAM RATS

Use Sundays to review work done during the week, rest and stay unique.

We have a beautiful life cuz I paid the price which was to repent/be nice.

If it's all music what's there to complain about?

Don't work--hold back strength. Cuz when the time comes you'll do nothing else: that's God's way.

Liberals aren't into laws: they are lawless. Ethics, morals and standards are gone but also no more solace.

Liberal equals contradiction. That's because their self-image (loving) opposes who they are: a fiction.

WOMEN CAJOLED TO ABORT AND DIVORCE!

Women cajoled to abort or divorce are called "good", "worthy" or "trendy" but end sadly or in poverty.

Of course they disbelieve it--it's followed by jokes. Media is mixed-up so people fall back to their yokes.

Rome: Control the masses by keeping them stupid and self-indulgent but none avoids punishment.

The evil is not in bread or circuses but the willingness to sell their rights as free men for food/games. Cicero

Full bellies/excitement of games distracts men from those needs which games can never meet.

Worlds collapse when evil takes over. From county to state we need a makeover, with full exposure.

"Heckler's veto": whoever yells the loudest wins by being annoying like a mosquito--not peace but ego.

There's a point where silence rules. You can't say a thing without offence so save yourself from fools.

DAM RATS

Freedom is like snow cones in hell. Without it man gets scared, no one cares, he's stuck in a shell.

Feminism ruined marriage. Women are taught to degrade their husbands, not nurturing: reality switches of witches.

If "they" don't know about it, it's "not happening". So instead of studying they're napping (it's baffling).

Movies reflect and create culture: a feedback. They guide us into destruction or provide resolution.

Someone writes a book then we have a whole new worldview and vocabulary seen as reality? Hope it's mine

SMILE OR YOU'RE MEAN, THE MEAN DON'T SMILE

The left thinks if you don't smile like the other fakes, you're mean--cuz smileys cover all bad things.

Most people want security in this world, not liberty. Henry Louis Mencken

Outa California liberal hell! The Utah kids are so nice and you never have to tell em twice.

Whenever liberals are in control illogic rules and they think it's cool as we're dictated to by fools.

Feminism made men the adversary--but protection from a good man is your only hope missy.

How to get through the latter days: Do your own thing--what you're born for--before it's too late.

Dogs sense weakness and people do too. How people act before you get strong is what pushes you.

It's the Fallen Hero Syndrome: When hero slips they all jump on the bandwagon and pull him down.

DAM RATS

The most intelligent are really bashed in this generation as the dumbed are compelled to aberration.

It's sick--the bathrooms and everything. The break from norms is all paganism even joyless flings.

Alex Jones is a leading genius of this generation. His glib takes on history and theory: wow, inspiration.

The Washington Post now writes the hit piece talking points for the rest.

The hypocrisy, arrogance and totally delusional Behavior characterizes fools going down, yes sir.

They believe in their desperateness if they throw each other overboard they will survive, no jive.

FAKE GLOBALIST MEDIA IS HATED (CNN +)

Fake Media is hated so much nothing they can do will ever put Humpty Dumpty together again.

The crazy Hillary/Pelosis are on fruitcake level power trips. So arrogant, mentally ill and fallen: ick!

With this kind of weakness, evil blindness and deadly ignorance the whole world is laughing at us.

I pray the old American spirit explodes as we fight the animating contest of liberty from toads.

They want to see their own president as a failure--how pathetic they are!

CNN overnight has a one-star lower-than-cable rating cuz they said our great president was failing.

People across the world are so sick of teleprompters and news garbage/slurs.

Since tyranny is the default setting in mankind, resistance is the animating contest making us divine.

DAM RATS

CNN is a filth hole with toilets overflowing. God always reveals things eventually--isn't it interesting?

They ended free speech in the name of not stirring them up: how globalists used Islam nonstop.

He's a tool for the democrats and the radical left. That's Paul Ryan a "republican" but a dirty rat.

Liberal logic can make you hazy but recall that Einstein said "am I, or all the others crazy?"

President Trump is a reprieve like Jonah being sent to Nineveh to give them a chance to repent.

HILLARY WOULDA BEEN THE END

Hillary would've been the end of free speech: mass arrests/huge wars making Hitler look tame.

People who hate Trump are the ones destroying us--treasonous chumps.

In a reprieve God gives nations time to repent--cultural psychology moves as a unit and slowly ascends.

In the times of Noah people were evil cuz they swam in evil waters, no?

This radical ideology is virulent, violent and seductive to millions of people (so we must fight it).

Societies go crazy en masse. It's pure groupthink [cultural psychology] that creates the ass.

The herd runs off the cliff. Think for yourself and ignore any rift.

God categorizes us, sinners from stars: All who want Satan, go there. All who want Me, be here.

God's giving them enough rope so they feel invincible then their mental illness comes out: have hope.

DAM RATS

After Hollywood bewitched the world many are parting from this falsehood, coming back into the fold.

I'm done posting the hellish headlines. I may have only a few days left and this time is mine.

After not seeing FOX for two months I saw it today but walked away cuz the urgent was downplayed.

They don't enforce, they complete the smuggling process. Everything's backward, a mess.

We will not find salvation with the controlled left as they've stolen the renaissance to destroy it.

Hillary says it's white folk's fault this happened. So no blame for going out and randomly killing em.

"We need to reform the police" as if it was their fault they got killed. People: think, please!

TARGETING GROUPS IS TERRORISM

When you target groups for killing, you're organizing terrorist attacks: these times are chilling.

We can't fight it when the public is so dumbed down. Alex Jones

Black males: The book gets thrown at em and they go to criminal school, lose power and family.

This is totally orchestrated to send em out in the streets to bring in federalization--not sweet.

Someone should've thrown tomatoes at a despicable performance of a race baiting president.

Too often we judge others by their worst examples and ourselves by our best intentions. George W. Bush

DAM RATS

She wrote "all lives matter" but then quickly deleted it. J-LO wants approval, can you believe it?

Race relations were very good before Obama took office. He triggered all of it, plus he's lawless.

It's been hell under Obama. Under this Marxist many got crazy, just gave up or got drunk/lazy.

The precariat is the new dangerous class. Monthly saved from poverty they vote for high tax.

"For the health of the mother" happens 2% of the time yet is used as excuse to abort 98% of the time.

Trump was the heavy while she resorted to tired, hollow platitudes and empty cliches with arrogant attitude.

LIBERALS CRAZY OVER WORDS NOT ACTIONS

Liberals are so dense their only concern is words not actions: "Trump's mean"/ignore destruction.

They're so arrogant in their emptiness, so haughty and superior and we're sick of this (soon we'll be outa this).

Gun Control Levels: 1. Increase background checks. 2. National registry. 3. Limit # of guns. 4. Confiscate guns/ammo.

The loving lawless sixties produced a bunch of old hippies who became unloving tyrannies.

The maximum tyranny is the level you'll accept, for once they get power you won't be able to object.

It's the in-thing to be lewd. It has no class, they're an ass, but it's social acceptance, alas.

Of course they're mentally ill, having bought that line. It's intended to do us in/make us unrefined.

DAM RATS

If they can ban anything they can ban everything. Stop giving into brainless kids you're enabling.

They paid two million to teach em how to throw fits about phantom racism that doesn't even exist.

It gives me pleasure to see liberal professors face to face with the monsters of which they're the creators.

Donald is a breath of fresh air. He wants to revive us--defend us--but not for money, he really cares.

We love the Donald cuz he rings a bell. He's obviously the only one who will end this hell.

Upstarts who arrogantly come against Donald, making fools of themselves; mental dwarfs.

The prayer of one good man changes a nation--that's what the bible says, so get prayin'

GENERAL PUBLIC IS DUMB AS HELL

The general public is so far removed from reality and history they could never understand this tragedy.

Your progeny are empty, worldly and misguided. Feminism--give me a break-- they are not unique, freaks.

I learned the safest place was So. Utah or N. AZ. Looked for a house in that area- -bingo, up came the best.

When there's so much happening just listen to Trump. He is true reality not a bunch of bunk.

The new age has brought us down while the old fashioned America aspired to be on top, renowned.

Like Nineveh, we could be reprieved! God was to judge, but changed His mind when they believed.

DAM RATS

Although a psychologist I have a master's in political science, it's fascinating to me: Political Psychology.

Most women don't study--they get their views from "The View" and crap like that: brainwash and silly chats.

Climate Change is an anti-human shutdown program for austerity--a weapon to cut off our energy.

GE's economic warfare 101: Shut down all competition so they can jack up prices with out carbon taxes.

Trump speaks the truth and no one else has that kinda juice--we need him: tell the youth!

We're stupid, were afraid, we have no vision. The whole culture's degraded so Jesus, start fishin'.

The animating contest is when you become your best fighting for liberty--it's your test.

CAN'T FIGHT FOR LIBERTY IF NEEDING APPROVAL

Before fighting for liberty, I was a worm--needed approval from evil people/rebuff made me squirm.

Trump will fix it, understand that. Those others are no-where compared to the King Brat.

To me the biggest result of liberty is privacy. To not be invaded by messers causing anxiety.

VA heads responsible for incompetency and abuse. I know the crap that went on there and it's obtuse.

Donald, we just love you. You give us hope, man--we're so tired of the lascivious liberal crew.

I used to be a liberal: no boundaries, lines nor morals too. That's the liberal mindset: pee-yoo.

DAM RATS

Why can't they go back to Syria after Putin clears out vermin? If they stay, we die especially our women.

False Christians are idiotic, saying "peace" to enemies when true victory comes from fighting.

Obama paid Iran 150 billion dollars to build nukes but vetoed spending for the troops. Oops.

Liberal feminists think if you don't agree with them, you don't count. It's "The View" you must discount.

It's the animating contest for your liberty once you see the social chicanery of the peanut gallery.

Unless they believe it in heart, Christianity seems absurd--thus persecution across the world.

ABSURD DEMANDS OF SOCIAL JUSTICE WARRIORS

Demands of social justice warriors have become SO absurd they're a joke—remove this yoke!

Went to FOX, how boring. They omit or plain out LIE so I have 10 hrs found time, spirit soaring.

It's a mind-control cult so watch out. It's insane--makes no sense--but keep to truth/have no doubt.

Constantly lowering the standards and dehumanizing the middle class: conquering through sin, fast.

Dictators hate the poets. They always target them cuz they cut to the chase so you know it.

Females tend to get their opinions from The View, neighbors and friends--these are dangerous trends.

Buzzwords: "Disturbing", hater, homophobe, racist, sexist—these are the words of the anarchists.

DAM RATS

FOX is flooded with leftism under the guise "fair and balanced" but I'm sick of this with no letup.

"Global Warming" is a scam and power grab to take over the energy industry and it means money.

In Liberalism there is no crime or punishment so him letting violent felons go is our predicament.

The silly students whine and scream as their "safe space" of not being offended is lamented.

Vindictive protectiveness describes the end of free speech on campuses by asses.

LEFT-RIGHT DIVISION IS EXPLODING

Liberals vs. conservative hatred is growing: "affective partisan polarization" unknowingly.

Any firings will only encourage the mobs of our university's mentally ill, from false theories instilled.

Veterans: Thank you for your service though the country's gone left and they're banning our weapons.

Whoever's for socialism (Bernie Sanders) or Lewdism (Hillary Clinton) kindly leave (unfriend).

We hate each other: the left vs. the right. We see them as dumb, cold and vile so we must fight.

Conservative Christians are targeted in schools, families and trust funds: persecution is NO FUN.

They wanna break us down and make us obey: accepting their insanity in dismay--a world so grey.

Egotistical brats wanting attention. One day in the spotlight and now no mention?

DAM RATS

Liberal illogic comes from finding moral equivalence between unequal forces--they justify asses.

Stay away from FOX news cuz they're not telling you the truth. Stick to the internet, be a sleuth.

When Muslims attack the left attacks victims: "Stop blaming Muslims and take a look at yourselves"

PC word battles instead of seeing clear and present danger. Could the students get any stranger?

LIBERALS ARE A PATHOLOGICAL HEX

The left's a pathological hex. The enemy is killing us and their chief concern is destroying/blocking critics.

Evil brattish children are being used to take us into extreme Pol Pot tyranny. You talk and they get leery.

Such a breath of fresh air leaving liberal bastion California, despite it's beauty and how it warms ya.

If it's the left call them out and pin them down. It's the left--say that always about the clowns.

There are many heteros who want to adopt but the sick liberals would rather abort.

Conservative principals are best for lifting women up--for women need freedom: fill thy cup.

We're told not to stereotype but we can and we MUST do it to carry on this lethal fight.

Pathological altruism: It's liberals and the churches who facilitate invasion by leeches.

How can you say we're like them! This shows your cold ignorance and lack of empathy, man.

DAM RATS

Colorado College just banned the words "Jesus, God and Lord": You just can't say these words.

Alex Jones is a brilliant genius of this generation. Haters just don't like the vital information.

One disaster after another, frenetic: It helps to see it as prophetic in order to not panic.

Trump divided families on Thanksgiving Day. Many had to leave the table they felt so betrayed.

AN ENTIRE GENERATION LOST HOW TO THINK

The entire generation lost how to think and the results of such mind-control will be a permanent stink.

We have the first amendment in this country no matter what the crazy college kids say.

Ignore the movie stars, for liberals are being shown for all the filth and deception they are.

This is a sick old hippy witch. They're all around and in total control as they lie (give you a pitch).

They say not to fear cuz they don't now what's going on. Don't listen to these loud lemmings, hon'

You know what it's like to be a pariah--when you speak your mind (though refined) they show paranoia.

If guns are outlawed only outlaws will have them and that's how liberal logic is flawed.

You wanna take our guns while letting those in who want to kill us? In you there is no justice.

Conservatives say "kill" those wanting to kill us. With liberals "don't hurt feelings" is their focus.

DAM RATS

The bible is about people standing up against tyrants. Not laying down but fighting/killing giants.

Whenever you feel lost, hopeless or sad, just think of Donald. Become one with his mission, be bold.

Those who think clearly see Donald was the only way out. He is so wise like an energy spout.

GENDER PRONOUNS AND OTHER DUMBS

"He" means "mankind"--a nonpersonal pronoun. Not "he and she"--that's just plain dumb.

Students threw paper airplanes at me when they saw I wouldn't always say "he and she" but just "he".

They celebrated immorality and persecuted righteousness. Blessings stopped and judgment was a mess.

Praise God! Trump was divinely equipped and in perfect health to be our next president.

By telling us not to criticize they crippled our thought and that's why all the lies we bought.

Felt like a stranger in a strange land around 'em. Couldn't take who they believed in, like Hillary Clinton.

Please help us Father, to make America great again! There's only ONE who can do it, amen.

Maybe your sin is something the culture approves of--even promotes. You'll still get old/ugly, folks.

Liberals find moral equivalence between all things and that's how they cause trouble/let in thieves.

Trump babes are wearing "Hillary for Prison" T-Shirts. Also, minorities are recent converts.

DAM RATS

The kids and their dumbed parents are Christophobic and to kindly Christian folk they are acerbic.

When the youth chasten free speech tell em to shut up. These commies wanna blow it all up.

There was little racism before our chief created radical divisions and it's all precursory to fascism.

2016: USA's best or worst year depended on elections: either prosperity or no more protections.

Trump is the only one. Minorities, women and even some reformed Democrats love him.

FEMALE COMMIES IN YOUR OWN FAMILY?

Some had Hillary or Sanders-lovers in their own family. What a horrible thing to endure, truly.

Trump hires women and puts them in prominent positions. Shut up detractors, stop fishin'.

So some ex-wife reports him as "frightening" and they come and get his guns— she's getting even.

The growing tyranny is terrible. California confiscating guns without calling AND banning ammo.

The Green Movement is phony (meant to ruin businesses) while the elites get all the money.

We're all gonna die so raise hell then die! We've been conquered by evil but God can still defy.

WORLD FAME, RENOWNED, RICH BUT OLD: A LIFE'S WORK

You can be cursed for decades and five days. It's *exact* then success released: your/His glory raised.

DAM RATS

Once things go smoothly at last, it's hard to believe and you expect less when actually that's all passed.

Genius must ignore the persecutory herd or be stressed with distain. Devotion to work brings gains.

She talks like she knows me but she has no idea (it's been years) so how does she know? It is calumny.

They're intimidated cuz they know you're better than them.

Victory: the day, hour and minute.

You couldn't have come this far to be dropped off to age and die. God has the Victory planned so don't cry.

The truth of God's timing should bring you great relief. He hasn't forgotten and you caught the energy thief.

Not enough to be good, gotta be fantastic. Competing with upper echelons, be strong/never break.

It's hard to say things simply but to talk too much is easy.

DAM RATS

I never stopped, I persevered, I overcame, I worked, I will succeed as God will bless me with Victory.

Sometimes God must shock us into compliance. That's why we love Him--He only hurts to enhance.

A DAM RAT

The Whoopie Incident

WHOOPI AND THE OPPRESSION HIERARCHY PYRAMID

To Whoopi, race means blacks and Mexicans not Jews or Asians since they're successful often.

What Whoopi said was antisemitic, racist, and downplayed the murder of 6 million people.

It's an attempt to ignore what happened 70 years ago, when we should never forget you know.

She's acting like it didn't happen or was a general thing not intentional mass murder of the Jews.

Hiding behind her race won't protect her nor will a scripted apology--this is too huge see.

DOWNPLAYING MASS MURDER

To ignore/downplay the mass murder of six million people is **BEYOND** evil/this will continue.

What about the millions of relatives of millions of murdered Jews--how do you think **THEY** feel?

This is the turning point for The View and hopefully liberal Whoopi too: feminist **KOOKS**.

Someone who is that antisemitic will always downplay their victimization, justify it or ignore it.

Whoopi marginalized the death of six million Jews, providing cover for Holocaust deniers too.

The Whoopi Incident

Hitler intended to annihilate every Jew on this planet and she dared to deny it? Makes ya sick.

Whoopi is forgiven by the Hollywood left cuz she's black and a progressive but we won't forget it.

The media supports the kooks, emboldening them to do crazy things and that is all it took.

They made it all about skin color and this is the result. It's the holocaust they don't know about.

APATHY VS. AWARENESS OF ENORMITY

Whoopi and most liberals don't understand the enormity of the greatest hate crime in history.

The greatest hate crime the world has ever seen liberals ignore because victims were white see?

Whoopi needs time off to view the stacks of dead bodies, the crematoriums, the cattle cars.

Along with Civics dropped from curriculums is education on the holocaust: learn it now ma'am.

The era of the fifties was very low key cuz people saw what could happen without God/decency.

Liberals became flippant & arrogant about it. Narcissistic, debauched, diverted into irrelevance.

Learn what seeing a swastika does to a survivor of the holocaust or every time they see a dog.

Berliners in the twenties were debauched as hell then look what followed: liberals need to know.

WAS SLAVERY RACISM OR INHUMANITY?

The Whoopi Incident

Was slavery not about racism but man's inhumanity to man? To generalize means no blame given.

It leaves victim's families with no resolution to the biggest mass murder from man's beginnings.

If Whoopi isn't fired we'll sink in our swill of ignorance but these realizations could also be a catalyst.

To The View everything is about race except the holocaust--what a ridiculous disgrace.

CRTs cannot acknowledge Jewish suffering since that undermines the hierarchy of oppression.

Top of oppression pyramid must be white--they cannot be the victims or how could they be right?

What does Whoopi think Hitler meant when he said "master race"? It was all about race you ass.

JUST A BUNCHA WHITES FIGHTING

How is this about race? Just a buncha whites exterminating six million other whites, ok?

I'm actually thrilled this has come out. As a student of the holocaust this is going to be a blowup.

Like someone seeing black-on-black crime saying "oh, it's just them, doing what they do", aye.

As we learn the enormity of the holocaust Whoopi's booboo is more despicable and she's toast.

We couldn't stand her all these years and now this is the last straw while also educating us all.

"Being black, race means a different thing to me", using your skin color as a cover again Whoopi?

The Whoopi Incident

They're far more offended by Joe Rogan's comments on covid then the rewriting of the holocaust.

To ignore the holocaust or not teach it is to rewrite it cuz it was that historically catastrophic.

Joy Behar: "I don't know Joe Rogan can be reformed" but Whoopi's mere apology indicates its so?

Whoopi actually did us a great service because now we see what Critical Race Theory is all about sis.

Critical Race Theory: Whites are incapable of being victims [even living to oppress each other?]

In the context of Critical Race Theory, who cares about white on white crime? They're the enemy.

A COVER FOR HOLOCAUST DENIERS

Critical Race Theory points out that whiteness is already racist just by it's color--how racist.

CRT allows you to lump Jews in with the rest of the evil whites like Nazis, serial killers, crazies.

And if a black or Hispanic is conservative, they too are white, just ask Larry Elder or other brights.

If you don't act or think right--whether you're black or Mex--you'll be put in the oppressor's box.

If you don't fall in line and spout these lies you're as a bad as a Nazi or worse, a white guy.

The color line of white and black is all that matters and everything else is irrelevant/whitewashed.

Whites sit at the top of the oppressor pyramid and nothing will change that, even this?

The Whoopi Incident

CRT foolishness: To maintain the hierarchy they include Nazis with Jews under umbrella of whiteness.

They ignore the grisly black-on-white murders in South Africa the same way-- it's irrelevant ok?

White sits at the top of the oppression pyramid like fat or sugar as toxic and deadly foods to avoid.

She doubled down on Colbert then gave a coerced written apology so Whoopie is still a phony.

THEY DON'T FORGIVE US FOR THE SLIGHTEST

We're supposed to forgive her sorry but if we transgress the line we're fired, canceled, homeless, aye.

Would Goldberg accept erasing the black experience in the horror of slavery? Haul Worth

Would blacks accept slavery seen as "man's inhumanity to man" not them as target of the atrocity?

Puppet Justin Trudeau is told by his handlers: "Say freedom makes you traitorous outsiders".

They've taken training wheels off and are in your face priming you by gaslighting your thoughts.

When you fight Nazis you are called Nazis. That's the way you're labeled in a liberal world see.

A soulless demonic sociopath and puppet doing what he's told and totally cut off from God.

A big sister gains total control like a dictator--who's to know any better, who even questions her?

In her total control she gets in with the attorney handling the will and screws that up too.

100 KAREN KELLOCK BOOKS

AFFINITY OR MISERY
AGELESS CORNUCOPIA
AMERICA AWAKE!
AMERICA'S DAFT ERA
ARTS OF PALEO FASTING
AUTOPHAGY ON CHEATERS
BACKSTABBING NEUROTICS
BETRAYAL TRAUMA
BOOMERS AND BROKENNESS
BOOT ON NECK
CHAMPION GUIDES
COMMIE NUTHOUSE
COMMIES
COMMUNIST SPIRIT
CONTAGION OF MADNESS
CONTAGIOUS MADNESS
CULTURE CLASH BASHED
DAFT LEFT
DAILY FASTARIAN
DAM RATS
DIVERSITY IS CRUELTY
E-RACE WHITE
EVIL FREAKS (Beyond Gross)
THE END OR A BEND?
FEMALE BULLIES AND FEMI-NAZIS
FEMALE CARNALITY
FEMALE DUMB DOWN
FEMALE POWER DRIVE
FEMINISM AND RUIN 1 & 2
FIX FOR MISFITS
FOOLS & TRAMPS
FREEDOM SPEAKING
FRENEMY ENABLER
FRENEMY LIAR
FRENEMY THIEF
FRENEMY TRAITOR
TRENEMY TYRANT
GENIUS IS HELD DOWN
GLOBALISLAM
GOD USES THE FLAWED
HAZE OF THE LATTER DAYS

THE HERD IN WORDS
HIX POLITIX
HOW THEY RUINED US
JUST SKIP DINNER
LE FEMME AND THE COMMUNIST SPIRIT
LIBERAL CHAOS & ROT
LIBERAL DOUBLETHINK
LIBERAL GALL 1 & 2
LIBERAL SHOVE-DOWNS
LOCK YOUR GATE
LOSERS and Femme Fatales
MANUAL FOR SUPERIOR MEN
MODERN ART FROM HELL
MOSTLY FAKE
NOTES TO CHAMPS 1 & 2
OVERCOME FRENEMIES
PC MAKES US CRAZY
PEOPLE ARE CRUEL
PEOPLE PROBLEMS 1 & 2
PERSECUTED GENIUIS
POLI-PSYCH MYSTERIES
PRETENTIOUS SLOBS
QUEEN BEE
RED NEW DEAL
RETURNING TO FIRST NATURE
SEASON OF TREASON
SEPARATE MEANS HOLY
SOCIAL HYPNOTISM
SOLITUDE SOLUTION
SUPERCILIOUS
THE SCHOOLS SCREWED EM UP
TOAD TO PRINCE
TRIALS CYCLES
TRUMP VS. GROUP
TRUST IN TRASH
THE TRUTH ABOUT PEOPLE
UNDERHEANDEDLY CLEVER
WALK TALL WITHIN WALLS
WE'RE NOT ALL ONE
WINNERS SKIP DINNER
WORK OR SMERK

KAREN KELLOCK PH.D.

M.S. Political Science, San Diego State. Ph.D. in Psychology, University of California Irvine. Postdoctoral: UCI School of Medicine, Dept. of Psychiatry [NIMH Grants]. Developed the Debris Theory of Disease, a theory of system pathology in 120 books and 22 textbooks for the general public. The theory has a general formula: All disease is obstruction, all recovery is elimination, all success is attraction. The three obstructions are people, habit and food. Remove obstruction and snap to your goals, waiting in the wings.